SUNDAY HOUSES THE SUNDAY HOUSE

WINNER OF THE IOWA POETRY PRIZE

SUNDAY HOUSES THE SUNDAY HOUSE

ELIZABETH HUGHEY

UNIVERSITY OF IOWA PRESS

IOWA CITY

University of Iowa Press, Iowa City 52242
Copyright © 2007 by Elizabeth Hughey
www.uiowapress.org
Printed in the United States of America
Design by Richard Hendel

The University of Iowa Press is a member of Green Press
Initiative and is committed to preserving natural resources.

Printed on acid-free paper

LCCN: 2006934476
ISBN-10: 1-58729-528-8
ISBN-13: 978-1-58729-528-7

07 08 09 10 11 P 5 4 3 2 1

FOR CHIP

A window across the river caught the sun

as if the miracle were working, on the wrong balcony.

—Elizabeth Bishop

CONTENTS

ONE

 SOUTH

Summer after summer, afternoon came upon the window
that somebody had forgotten to close. It was a cab that took
the first cool breath of seven o'clock. The streets were like corners,
a modest variety of light. On the other side of thirty minutes,
he remembered the black luggage. To travel linked to the history
of unraveled lawns. Large country gliding along through brick houses,
angular trees. Now the yellow nightfall. The tablecloth lit
as though another South had decided to pick up the open sky.

VERONICA

How you took eyeliner and rouge and made your face into a tea saucer. Dark peonies heavy with tea. The way your face became a seated tango with a little mascara and the shadow that flies over the fields of Nebraska. I like how you took your lipstick and created an entire red pub with two drunks sleeping in separate booths. I can see in your powdered cheeks the yellow tooth of the polar bear, a zoo bear, in Alabama, anesthetized and dreaming, twitch of the whisker, paw slowly scooping a fish. Forget me not the beads that circle your neck, slip down your back, double spine, and go mousing across the floor to the wall socket that is not yet obsolete but not all modern and bewondering.

Some of the sixteenth century, as represented by snatches
of Benedetto Rinio's *History*, was rather botanic. At an
herbarium lined with floodwater, an elder can still hear
the occasional eruptions of spindle berries. The sixteenth
century is addressing an entire generation of plantsmen,
shouting, Hi! Hi! across the valley of 1485. Look at each
year in costume — 1511, 1533, 1555 — ever-rounded, herbal,
discussing those trees, their cousinships with paneled doors.

 HOW MUCH LONGER

Before I know the names of the existing,
I am looking for a new bird. The Goodhawk,

the Noblenut, my funny bird pinned
to the road, a new city. My feelings

about maps and shadows are so similar.
Noun verb the adjective, adjective noun.

That is a car ride. I feel about parades
what I feel about skipping pages.

Prayerfowl, Luck Jay, Blame Finch.
There are many ways and many reasons

for the world. The cow lows a new milk
in torrents into the pail. A field of eggplants,

a factory of basketballs. Let's not be sad
about vegetables. If there were no births,

and all things were mined, like blue
cabbage, marble, the coal miner

bringing soot-blackened lambs from below.
Once you have spoken, twice I have heard.

I come in from the snow to find a new family in the living room, a
smaller dog at a different bowl. I rub the cat, and a child appears:
Welcome, Son. You were born the day I first thought of you, in a
square, in Spain, after black rice. I shopped for gifts. You wanted
a compass held by pirates. You needed it. Would I please buy it
for you. In customs I said, *My son has to have that farmer's cheese. He
deserves the blue tulip.* But the guards kept it all. I have nothing. And
I am going to live this whole thing backwards next time. Poppies
will fold and slide into the soil. Royalty will move into museums
before they take them down and return the stones to the quarry.
After years of eating saffron, I will know nothing about saffron.

Those who have given birth, and those who have been born.
Those who fear birds, and those who watch them.
Who can't say no. Those who wear watches, and those
who stop people on the street. Those who give up the world,
and those who perform household duties. Who names, who faces.
Those who hang up their clothes. Who worry about weight.
Worry about teeth falling out in public. Fear deep water. Fear birds.
Those who hold the door, and those who let the branch fly back.
Eat the wafer, eat the flesh. Those who play the woman,
and those who play the man. Who might as well.
Who lost their chance. Who lift their shirts. Who take it out
on their pets. Bargain. Never ask. Those who know their neighbors,
and those who can't speak to squirrels. Who hang up,
who have to repeat. Who hang themselves,
and who sip. Who have one great night of anonymous sex,
and those who take the last piece. Are never really alone.
Are unattached to outcome. Who mop every night.

 GOOD NIGHT '73

Now we know that the gin drinks do not matter.
That grown daughters call their mothers around midnight
from under poolwater. Smoking in bed. What is behind
the door marked by the potted fir is not memorable,
but to have such lines on wallpaper in a hallway,
raincoat yellow, sliding down like firemen
on poles in a dish liquid commercial on mute.
This is how to make a day end for a long time.
To fall asleep mid-moisturizer, hands above the head.
Tamper with sleep until you get it right,
and wake with shadow on the lids, as if blown there.

NO ONE NEED INVITE THE ANT

Hibiscus makes her own bee
out of stamen and pollen. Sea

takes an hour to bring the wave.
One breadfruit falls, and I am

cut down. Then another,
and I understand. Coal

is not coal by blackness
but by the fire burned clean.

When I move I fling chunks
of light onto everything.

Bubbles blown into the sand
made the sea, but why cause

the earth, why water, why dogfish.
Light moving from lantern to sky

to lantern. That is a day.
Larva twists in the beekept wax,

keeping warm the sweet in the mind
that knows honey. The ox

bumping against the sugarcane.
The boat tipping this way and that.

HOUSEWIFE

In the neighborhood people were turning off their TVs. I was walking home when her shadow covered me like squid ink. We said, *Nobody helps me pick up around the house. By the time I finish cleaning, it's time to start cleaning.* At night when I put myself to bed, she stays up in front of the TV, her eyes exchanging blues with the screen, folding even the cobwebs and stacking them on the couch. She is gone by morning, for errands, I guess. Tonight on my way to the bathroom, I pass her in the den. She says, *This is the first time I've been able to sit down all day.* I take her hand and bring her to bed. She says nothing. Her foot bumps mine like a cavefish under the covers.

TWO CAN PLAY

The carpool honks until the car turns blue then slips up the street without my son. I take a bus with him in my lap. Outside on green hills, goats bleat so loud they jump backwards. Now at the riverbank, *That one is a tugboat*, I say. He nods and his cap falls to the water, into the wake. *That is a cruise ship.* We get on and walk sideways through the crowd of people who are missing work and school. *Should I feel bad*, he asks. (Last night, at bedtime, my son took off his lips and hurled them at me. I rubbed softly away his eyes. He slept like a blank coin and missed his ride.) No, I say. *This is why I brought you here*, opening my change purse, but our conversation is cut short. Someone has lost their dog, calling, *Ritzie! Ritzie!*

Who spent the night for church the next day.
Stay Fredericksburg. Every room opens
to Kathy. The heart from homestead.
The map to go too far. Says Sunday house.
Says womanly opposite. Says glass armchair.
I'd like to cover the whole thing with rhinestone.
The guest downstairs, unframed, whose
background is reflected in the silver.
Make the bed as Victorian as a stack of soap.
Brick house adding fragrance to the mint.

When the 1960s were knocked down, I minded dreadfully the wounds of the countryside, the uniformed mansions about out of drawing rooms, the inheritance of over 10,000 rural surprises. All buildings were faced with honey-colored hamstone, trying to remind the supermarket of the Iron Age. Gardens hid behind bigger gardens. Unlike a 14th century sheep farm, granite nearly didn't end up in the modern world. It spawned smaller versions of itself inside notes, handwritten in ink, dealing with the only curb that encompassed the seedbed of ideas for a sustainable autumn.

TO BE SCATTERED ACROSS THE LAWN

I

Like a boat slipped free from the dock,
fog removes a cardinal from a branch.
The vacuum next door,
the pine in the window,
a man yelling *fuck you* from the street,
prevent my body from dissolving.
A baby crying *mama* keeps my arms
from flying free of my chest
to settle on the ceiling with a moth.

As one lamp is lit in Barcelona,
I'm lit. If one bison exhales . . .
I sit in a leather chair that's on carpet
that is on wood on cement on dirt,
and when I forget iron, all the nails
go back to where they came from.
The house clatters down,
leaving a flag hoisted above the rubble,
and the radiator laboring on its side.

2

Is it possible we may have to start again?
Laying down the roads,
blueprinting the bridges.
We get up and things have fallen into place.
The oven upright,
the fern in the corner.
A stone wall awakens two centuries of grass.
The iron and the oven discuss frost.
The fridge and the window, flight.
The nature of the washing machine
matches the train's,
but there is nothing
for the buzzer and the whistle
and the back and the forth.

TWO

 WHAT BIRD

Bulbs, gravel, driveway.
I had hyacinth on my mouth.
The city, without thinking,
will arrive with photographs.
Or it could, even in winter,
tap at the glass, at the birdbath,
to be asked to speak.

EGG, EGG

The simplest way to be tender is to
drop whatever you wish in a little pan.
It will be tenderer of course to wait
for about three minutes. The result
will be tender like some kind of
lace newspaper. Trustworthy, French.
Delicate fish the size of new peas
school and flow outward (I don't
know why I said this. It is true.),
on and on, in almost as many
variations as there are minutes before.

THE ARCHITECT AND THE ENGINEER

A TELEPHONE PLAY

Ask light what it wants to be.

        Ask metal to behave like glass.

Let the elderly pick the park benches.

        And the children the drinking fountains.

The hand is made

        for the elbow and arm.

The hips, with starship scope,

        direct the feet.

Where do the legs begin?

        In the waist.

What if trees hung from clotheslines?

        And dirt cleaned itself.

An antler, an artichoke.

        A strawberry, a heart.

Most of us fall somewhere between exact symmetry

        and complete disorder.

The solar planet

        and the polar sea.

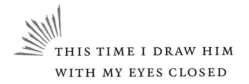

THIS TIME I DRAW HIM
WITH MY EYES CLOSED

Don't worry about ears. Intuit the nostril. The heart ends up
outside of the body, a second one, unfastened and brimming,
labeled everything. There it goes, up one shoulder and down the
arm. Leaving the paper, now it is in the field, now the
scratchflower. Geese cross the pond. Now, we talk about the
geese. Now, we talk about the poem about the geese. How they
do not mean to cast their image on the water. Nor does the water
mean to hold the image of the geese.

LIT THROUGH THE NIGHT

It snowed. It was mid-May,
so the sharp, and the red-orange,
the sandy. Since 1919 was
a home farmed in the temple
like bluffs into every Spring,
then the new trail lives hours
to the east. We make
our climate, grow cotton
along the terraces
more than twice as long
as every place to hide.

A ONE AND A

In another room, on the other side of the country, even without speaking, you are apologizing to me. On this day in America, we all sit down to eat at the same time. Every chair in every restaurant is taken. Our mouths chew in the shapes of closed-lipped words: *I am sorry. You look good. When you die, I want you to go to heaven.* Then, the sound of caws from our chair legs as we push back from the table and go on. In the museum, portraits of stern men slip off their canvases onto the faces of girls. They'll be the judges, they say. I apologize for things I wanted to do but didn't, for what I have done, will do, and what I can't remember I did. With that, the party that I skipped eight years ago finally ends. Tony wakes in the kitchen chair, Adam calls a taxi, Katherine takes off her purple dress, and Dave and Allison move to Austin with their terrier.

VERONICA

There are plenty of koi snorting in the pond. Get all the blankets
into the yard. We are having the picnic of our lives. I need a knife
longer than my finger but shorter than that tree limb above your
head, the one with the leaf on it and a lark clearing the throat
from his air. Let's go again. Pretend we have not eaten. Fill all
sorts of hungers with the teeny crumpet in your palm. The pond
is behaving as predicted by the weatherman who said the pond
will remain in the ditch and the koi in the pond and the worm in
the koi and your head on your neck. My feet were warm when he
said it about 99 degrees, and my earlobes held the most precise
chill as if for a minute all the temperatures the day would be were
resting there waiting to come and go. 65 and 39 and 40. I believe
it is 43. Have another blanket. The tea is cooling. I hear a koi
bumbling in the thermos. I believe your stole has mated with
mine. Let's split the offspring for dinner. Soufflé and picnics
don't go but neither do hats and bull's-eyes and look all around
you.

MY PARTY

A girl only gets so many parties.
Did you see my shoes? Did anyone

notice my shoes? I wish I were
drunk. When I shop for friends,

I shop drunk. Will someone get over
here and talk to me? I like sand dollars.

I like black pearls. I tried lipstick
but I could not determine

where the lip ends and the nose
begins. Where's the cake?

This is not my party anymore.
It is the party's party. This is

the partiest party in the party party.
Scotch squats in a crystal decanter

like a man in a dress. Even the perfume
eats with pinkies. I want to go home,

because the party has elected,
as a group, without words,

like a herd of moths, to celebrate
something else. Taste buds.

The end of all work. No. For one
moment, one thought bloomed

in each head: nobody wanted
to be someplace else. The men

forgot about the game. The slim
minnow of lust left the bellies of boys.

One woman faced the window
and fit a whole tea sandwich

into her mouth like a bedspread
into the dryer. Even the waiter

slicing the roast carved a thick
piece in the likeness of his father.

COUNTRY SONG

The rain, even before the clouds have darkened,
has already fallen. Leaves, too. When I received a letter
from you, I had already read it. Night has already turned
to day, and day to night. Cake, when just flour and egg,
has already been sliced and spread across many tongues
like air, which going in is really heading out, as are rolling
curlers into hair. Nail polish, even when still in the jar,
has chipped and scattered, a flake in the supermarket, a fleck
in the sink, several caught in clothes, run through the washing
machine and drained into the creek behind our house,
which we've already left. Before we met, our children
were asking for more milk and had grown. When we met,
love was already there, but I hadn't stopped loving you.
You were already gone, but I still loved you.

George said that before I met him he used to stay indoors
drinking red wine with the curtains drawn on weekdays when he
should have been at work. It is true. I walk back through the
years, knock on George's door, and find him on the couch,
candles dripping beneath a tapestry of the Tree of Life in which a
canary sings to a sleeping hedgehog. I drink the wine. I sit on the
couch. I tell him that soon his girlfriend's dad will come over and
get him out of here. They will break up, but a redhead will come
after. Giving in to an ultimatum, George will marry on an island.
They'll have a baby named after a common flower. Some hot
nights, George will sleep naked on the kitchen floor. It gets pretty
bad again after that, so I tell him that I'll stop for now. He says to
get from his apartment to a cornfield, you have to do much more
than go left.

LONG PLAYING RECORD

I met a girl with a practical beauty.
She said, *I can do it.*
I said, *I'd like to see you try.*
I can hold a conversation
while carrying a to-do list.
This girl, though, can speak
two words at the same time.
I say, *You will be my friend now,*
but there is a method for that.
The last time I made a friend,
a friend did it for me.
I've been walking into parties
with other people for decades.
The teenager strums his guitar
in the pizza parlor, forever.
To be wanted, to be two-wheeled
and created for use. I want
to be trapped in happiness,
the fig that escapes death.
This time last year, a whisper
turned to pipe smoke in my mouth.

 WORK POEM

I find joy and accomplishment in the alphabetized arena.
This is not about the two of us, boss.
This is in regards to all working relationships.
The shipper, the shipment, and the shipped to.
The cleaner, the cleanliness, and the cleaned.

Now I am a housekeeper.
I'd like to be a chickpea to know
how it feels to roll under the stove.
I know those aren't real birds I hear.
That, though, is a real sock.
I am a little scared to make the bed.
You never know when you get up
in the morning if you will return again.
The world, in that way, is a tomb.
The cantaloupe grows into its netting.
The bird grows into its crosshatched song.
The broccoli head is studded with nightingales.
Wind does not come through the window in cubes.
It twists like a torso and catches the canvas on my feet,
and I can do my work at one more mile per hour.

Take a right out the door.
At the top of the hill, turn left at the Laundromat.
Inhale fabric softener, exhale smoke.
The sidewalk turns to peach skin.
Pass the value butcher.
Pass the man with teeth missing.
Now you feel perfect.
Compare yourself to the vegetable mart with dry gourds.
Compare yourself to the car wash.
To the hair clasp on the sidewalk.
You are better than that.
Join the passing foot race.
Take off your shirt.
Take a sports drink from the sideline.
Go wherever you wish.
Get change. Pee behind a Volvo.
The wrecked world is mending itself like a starfish.

In the mornings, I am handmade, but by naptime, I'm full of screws. I stop by the secretary, and she says, *I am the executive assistant!* I am Biz Dev. When a Biz Dev rides the elevator from the Banker's Heart to the Summit Club, basement workers grab their coats. Every workplace is a factory. If this desk were an assembly line, then this typing would be making a product. Like a thermos? No, like a campaign for aspirin. I wish I had a stapler to attach this gum wrapper to this receipt for a bowl of noodles I ate in Vancouver. God, you have such a poor work ethic. Cobble me a motorbike and I will rev it in the break room.

SON ON A HILL

I can't see my son anymore.
He is so tiny,
the size of a pencil dot.
In the shopping mall,
I find a new son.
A black man in a baseball cap
looking at telephones. Son, I say,
because I am your mother, that's why.
I've missed you, he says.
We leave and drive back to the house.
Look, kitchen, I've found him.
See how little it takes to make a nose.
An angle is all. A dot for an eye.
Dear god, Son, you are growing by octaves.
You are getting too big for this lap,
for this room, for this street!
A siren splits the day into two lungs.
One inflates and drifts out over
the backyard. Go on, I say, and there
he goes. A tulip droops around noon.

HAILSTORM

A horse wading in water
at seven thirty
in summer
after a storm.
An intersection
full of hail
knucklesized
in July. Hail
in a vegetable garden,
before peas,
before breakfast.
A hot rod nosing
a pile of hail.
A man waking
before dawn to pray.
The place where the body
first enters the breath.
Dawn and power
racing for light.
The base of the nose,
the top of the throat.
Refrigerator shudder.
Pop of fish eggs
in a turtle mouth.
Tadpole turning
in a puddle of hail.
A house up the street
coming on again.
A repairman in a yellow jacket.
A grandmother rising
from her recliner,
slept there by mistake.

 THREE

SUBJECTS NOT SUITABLE FOR AUTOFOCUS, FUJI INSTRUCTION MANUAL

LOVE, BY GUY DE MAUPASSANT

Very shiny subjects (*This glacial hour of dawn.*)

Subjects photographed through glass (*Our hut, in the shape of a cone, looked like an enormous diamond with a heart of fire which had been suddenly planted there in the midst of the frozen water of the marsh.*)

Subjects that do not reflect well, such as hair or fur (*And inside we saw two fantastic forms, those of our dogs, who were warming themselves at the fire.*)

Subjects with no substance, such as smoke or flames (*The sky was, in fact, beginning to grow pale, and the flights of ducks made long rapid streaks which were soon obliterated by the sky.*)

Dark subjects (*I hear a voice, the voice of a bird. It was a short, repeated, heart-rending lament; and the bird, the little animal that had been spared, began to turn round in the blue sky over our heads, looking at its dead companion which I was holding in my hand.*)

Fast moving subjects (*As if that passing cry which is carried away by the wings of a bird is the sigh of the soul from the world!*)

Crossing the street without looking in each direction.
Crossing diagonally with more than one hatbox.
Running into the street to catch objects thrown from bus windows.
Standing on chairs or insecure stepladders.
Vacationing on cruise ships if unable to swim.
Careless behavior in steel mills and furnaces.
Crossing the street sobbing on hands and knees.
Using tricycles, push mobiles, or roller skates on the highway.
Crossing the street in artificial snow while being filmed.
Lying supine in a nightie after swallowing a handful of pills.
Playing in leaf piles after 1949.
Handling firearms when in doubt.
Climbing into a volcano.
Loitering around quicksand.
Sleeping in tunnels. Picking up snakes.

Walking home from the supermarket, I encounter five picnicking youths who appear to have consumed several bottles of wine. The heavy-lidded young lady casts a look at one of the young men. She has more to offer than oranges. Further on, two women on the sidewalk make plans while a boy cries at their feet. I suggest they stop this. Stopping the noise, though, will not stop the sadness. Looking closely, I can still see the outline of a *fuck you* from this morning. It smells of aftershave and sounds like a man walking two dogs. By sunset, his cigar will be gone, but the smoke will stain the teeth for good.

THOUGHT POLICE

I can't tell a Wednesday from a Thursday,
but I have come so far and never left myself,
remembering, always, what I was before I was born.

January seventh, I breathe out more than I take in.
My mouth takes the last photo on the roll:
Ganges, the gown I wear for brushing my hair,

peignoir, the white gown. Between the movies
and dreams, I am barely in front of myself.
I don't move the furniture when I sweep the silt.

Nothing is left unfucked in this world. Kiss,
then move mountains into the living room,
call the kids in for supper. The kiteflyer holds

the currency of air in two fingers. I play the woman
as cool as an open refrigerator, looking anywhere but where
I am going. I have to be told everything at least twice.

White is searching for the egg.
Green can't find a leaf.

Heat hovers around the empty
fireplace. Ring above the phone.

Moth deflates its wings and wraps
like a child out of the bath.

Dogless, a bark is in the mouth
of a cave. I am sitting

on the dock. Scent of bacon
flies by. Wasp of gardenia,

but there is no gardenia. Sun
is setting when the brown

of the lake settles on the water
like a blown bed sheet.

A sailboat. It sails.

How can I be sure that before cut open the lime is not filled with light? That when whole and on the branch, its insides aren't casinos walled in sequins, green plinking of money, lime-pitch smoke. At night in the forest, when all the light has crawled into another county on elbows and knees, the ground peels itself from the earth and wraps a tree trunk like a bag around a beer bottle. Even in your town, on a moonless night, when the windows look inward, like the other side of the skin, the driveway may become water, and the tree dive in, touch the other side of the globe, and spring back into place.

SON AT THE SWIMMING POOL

Are we on the golf course or in the pool?
he asks. That is a tough one.
I call on Swami Vivekananda:
We came to enjoy;
we are being enjoyed.
Son says being good
is not so easy. I agree.
It can't be helped.
There is a contest for diving
into the water, but nobody
has made climbing out
any more beautiful.

SWAMP CACHE

One tupelo harvest Smiley awakes in the middle of the heavy, dark seventies. The menus are crowded with crawfish. Smiley drives by the high school until eleventh grade shifts to endless sandy shallows. He remembers his oysterman's fingers, phasing out of bivalves and into 1987. Easing up the Emerald Coast by barge, drop by drop, soaking up pools of aftershave, Smiley moves his blinking road sign into the soft fluff that is the tupelo flower.

HEAVENLY BODIES GO IN CURVES

Applecarts in a tidy hotel
in London at a dinner
honoring brief hands
were still. Fingers
left the universe.
One side we call One Side.
We call the other
That Great Face.
Forget language.
A square . . . a square
will not go in an Englishman.
At such and such,
the apple will be questioning
a curvilinear world
and challenging gentlemen
to get rid of glory.

The rush to water continues.
64 teenagers crosswalk
across California.
A blue-ribbon, James.
The Great Lakes,
Richard. Donna says,
We actually tried to find
the arcane nuances
of clean water.
What they found
in storm drains
was beachwater
wracked with San Diegans.
The ocean ends up
in coffee cups
every time it rains.

INTERSECTION OF OAK AND LINDEN

I

When the fruit seed grows into a skyscraper,
when the toll booth converts to opera house,
the buzz saw early Saturday morning wakes
the neighborhood and the neighbors take their
toolboxes to the corner to begin building a new house.

There is nothing I can say
to change the purpose
of a building. No gestures for
the broad strokes of the bulldozer.

If sunlight were cement
then the ground would be speckled
in the coarse gray palms
of sunlight. The pick ax up against
the tree. Some days it seems this place
is just combinations. The aster
is one part wood, one part skin.

A road is half stone and half memory.
A body has the most sides of anything.

And when you combine the acorn squash
with a sea lion, you get a bird, actually,

you get wings and a tiny beak
and a smaller heart but wings.

2

We are speaking of the Vatican
and how you can't tell the weather
by that sky, is it flame blue or ice blue.

I mistook the change in weather
for a change in myself. I think I can tell
by one brick that the building was made to protect

the exotic plants through the winter: Wet-Tongued
Violet, Feather Faced Lily, Wax Betty. Then,
because of the flowers, there had to be music,

and the note was hoped to mate with a frond,
but the cello does not play with its own fingers,
and the lemon tree does not live on lemons.

3

When stacked bricks and rolled insulation,
the house. When brown branch and blossom,
nest. When blue corn and cotton, Kentucky.

The land is brindled with creeks and roads.
I am not the architect of anything. I am the life
made better. The color broken from the rocks.

The belly print in the grass. When the cello,
two centuries blush on my cheeks. When
the cigarette, leaves unroll into wide brown

flappings, reflected in apartment windows,
and a man shaving dips his razor, and
sinkwater rings like a telephone.

NOT TO MENTION THE TREES
COMING UP TO MY WAIST

A twigleaf:
    Watch it go into the seam of sleep where you are fishing.
Selected examples:
    May 7: Around four thirty, four minutes flew past my ear.
    May 13: Four mistakes.
    May 17: Now comes somersault four.
    May 25: I lost the canoe.

VERONICA

I know that day. That is the day a man crossing the park found a bottle of gin hidden beneath a bush and in one swig turned his chest into a bedroom slipper, fur-lined and foot-warmed. Not a day that birds sang with their feathers, only an occasional dagger of song. Every apartment building was attached to an apartment building. I caught a calendar page on my tongue. I am no across-the-room beauty. I am the dark side of a sequin. My dimple behaves like a reflecting pool. That day, my hair grew right into her style, *brioche mousseline*. No time to wet it down, I took her boots and went as Veronica to the New Year's party. We never seemed to get around to midnight.

Rhododendron, vacuum, rhododendron
boxwood, tight-end, boxwood
magnolia, recliner, magnolia
monkey grass, chest of drawers, grass
walnut, carport, walnut
clover, record player, walnut
daffodil, labrador, daffodil, yellow lab
blue jay, blue van, daffodil
pecan, living room, pecan
pansies, just kidding, pansies,
wood duck, tight-end, just kidding
hydrangea, heirloom, hydrangea
evergreen, squirrel, evergreen, squirrel
kudzu, yonder, kudzu
azalea, ready, azalea, okay
lenten rose, surgarless, lenten
dogwood, David, dogwood
hydrangea, someday I'll tell you about
hydrangea, boxwood, doorbell
boxwood, azalea, nightgown, azalea
crepe myrtle, aspic, crepe myrtle
clover, wasp in the pool, clover
black ant, it's ready, black wasp
cardinal, I'll get it, crepe myrtle
crocus, your ride's here, crocus
violet, spraynet, violet
hickory, bunt, hickory
sumac, Indian head, sumac
David, dogwood, David.

ACKNOWLEDGMENTS

Thanks to the editors of the following journals where some of the poems in this book first appeared: *Birmingham Poetry Review*, *The Hat*, *Shampoo*, and *Vanitas*.

I am also very grateful to the following people for their guidance and support: Jan and Jim Hughey, Jim Hughey III, Dara Wier, Jim Tate, Peter Gizzi, Lisa Beskin, and, most of all, Chip Brantley.

The Iowa Poetry Prize & Edwin Ford Piper Poetry Award Winners

1987
Elton Glaser, *Tropical Depressions*
Michael Pettit, *Cardinal Points*

1988
Bill Knott, *Outremer*
Mary Ruefle, *The Adamant*

1989
Conrad Hilberry, *Sorting the Smoke*
Terese Svoboda, *Laughing Africa*

1990
Philip Dacey, *Night Shift at the Crucifix
    Factory*
Lynda Hull, *Star Ledger*

1991
Greg Pape, *Sunflower Facing the Sun*
Walter Pavlich, *Running near the
    End of the World*

1992
Lola Haskins, *Hunger*
Katherine Soniat, *A Shared Life*

1993
Tom Andrews, *The Hemophiliac's
    Motorcycle*
Michael Heffernan, *Love's Answer*
John Wood, *In Primary Light*

1994
James McKean, *Tree of Heaven*
Bin Ramke, *Massacre of the Innocents*
Ed Roberson, *Voices Cast Out to Talk
    Us In*

1995
Ralph Burns, *Swamp Candles*
Maureen Seaton, *Furious Cooking*

1996
Pamela Alexander, *Inland*
Gary Gildner, *The Bunker in the
    Parsley Fields*
John Wood, *The Gates of the Elect
    Kingdom*

1997
Brendan Galvin, *Hotel Malabar*
Leslie Ullman, *Slow Work through
    Sand*

1998
Kathleen Peirce, *The Oval Hour*
Bin Ramke, *Wake*
Cole Swensen, *Try*

1999
Larissa Szporluk, *Isolato*
Liz Waldner, *A Point Is That Which
    Has No Part*